# CREATE YOUR OWN
# MAGAZINE
## BARBARA TAYLOR

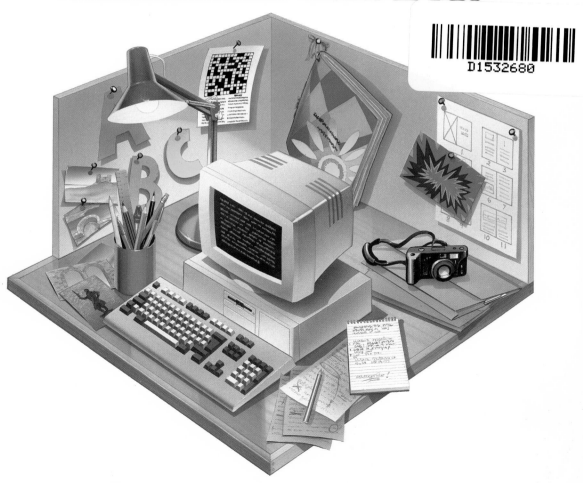

Sterling Publishing Co., Inc.   New York

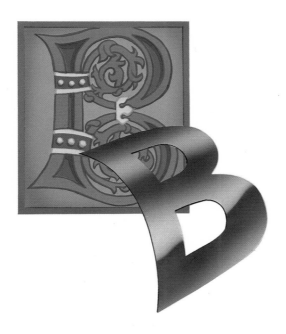

**Library of Congress Cataloging-in-Publication Data Available**

**Illustrator:** Brett Brandon
**Design:** Celia Hart
**Commissioning Agent:** Debbie Fox
**Copy Editor:** Diana Russell
**Series Design:** David West
Children's Book Design

10 9 8 7 6 5 4 3 2 1

Published 1993 by Sterling Publishing Company, Inc.
387 Park Avenue South, New York, N.Y. 10016
Originally published in Great Britain by
Simon & Schuster Young Books Ltd
© 1993 by Simon & Schuster Young Books
Distributed in Canada by Sterling Publishing
$^c/_o$ Canadian Manda Group, P.O. Box 920, Station U
Toronto, Ontario, Canada M8Z 5P9
Printed and Bound in Belgium

Sterling ISBN 0-8069-0425-9

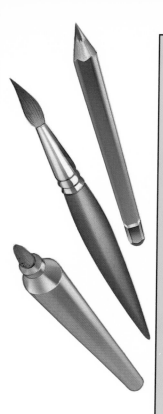

# CONTENTS

# WHY CREATE A MAGAZINE?

Do you like writing stories, doing puzzles, making things? Are you good at drawing or organizing information? Do you care about important issues? If your answer to any of these questions is yes, why not create your own magazine? It's fun to do and will help you understand how real magazines are put together.

The magazines in shops are created by teams of people and you will find it easier to create your magazine if you ask some friends to help.

**THE COVER**
pages 30–31

**THE WORDS**
pages 12–17

**THE PICTURES**
pages 18–23

## MAGAZINE ...          OR BOOK?

Here are some of the most important differences between books and magazines:

| MAGAZINE | OR BOOK |
|---|---|
| ★ comes out each week or month. | ★ only one made, but may be part of a series. |
| ★ usually a few pages with a paper cover. | ★ often lots of thick pages with a hard cover. |
| ★ has lots of pictures, especially cartoons. | ★ may have pictures, but words use up more space. |
| ★ can have stories, facts, puzzles, things to make. | ★ usually all facts or all stories. |
| ★ words and pictures by many different people. | ★ words and pictures by one or two people. |
| ★ often has free gift. | ★ a free gift is unusual. |

## YOUR IDEAS NOTEBOOK

It's a good idea to carry a small notebook around with you so you can jot down ideas whenever they come into your mind. You can divide up the notebook into sections, such as quizzes, cartoons, stories, competitions, places to visit and so on. This will make it easier to find your ideas later.

Spot the mistakes
— soccer game

How many tigers hidden in the jungle?

Haunted House maze —can you escape without meeting the ghost?

Which spaceship is the odd one out?

**THE DESIGN**
pages 24–29

**THINKING UP IDEAS**
pages 8–11

**FROM START TO FINISH**
pages 40–41

# THINKING UP IDEAS

Magazines can be about all kinds of things, from sport, computers and the environment to fashion, food or local news. Some magazines are linked to television programs or the characters in books. Many children's magazines are more general and include a mix of puzzles, interviews, cartoons, games and things to make.

Comics are magazines full of cartoons which tell stories. The first ones were called "funnies" and were collections of comic strips from newspapers.

## JOURNALISTS AT WORK

People called journalists write the articles in magazines. They go out to interview people and often specialize in one area such as news or sport. Journalists often use information sent by computers or faxes from all over the world. This helps to keep magazines up-to-date.

WHAT SORT OF MAGAZINE?

Wild life   Fashion   Cooking
Green Issues
Sport — soccer   Cartoon comic
       — tennis
       — baseball   Computers
Transport — trains
          — bikes   Mixture of things
          — cars
Making things

Jokes and riddles

crosswords   interviews

things to make

Puzzles

Make a list to help you decide the sort of magazine you want to create.

Telephone Directory

PLACES TO VISIT

ROAD ATLAS

Reference books will help you find places to visit and check facts.

## What will our magazine be like?
- How big will the pages be?
- How many pages?
- What will it be about?
- Will it be in color or black and white?
- Who will do the work?
- Where will we get the paper, pens and other equipment from?
- Where and when will we work on our magazine?
- Who will read it?
- How many copies shall we make?

PICTURES

**Cut out pictures or collect leaflets to give you ideas for topics or illustrations.**

## QUESTIONS AND ANSWERS

Before you decide what to put in your magazine, carry out a survey of the people you hope will read it, to find out what they want. Make up a list of questions and ask as many people as you can, so that you get a mixture of opinions.

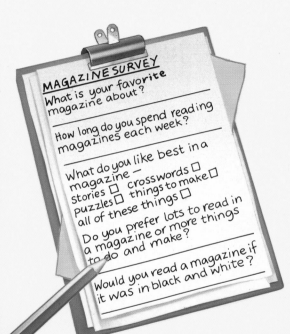

MAGAZINE SURVEY
What is your favorite magazine about?

How long do you spend reading magazines each week?

What do you like best in a magazine —
stories ☐  crosswords ☐
puzzles ☐  things to make ☐
all of these things ☐

Do you prefer lots to read in a magazine or more things to do and make?

Would you read a magazine if it was in black and white?

You could draw up a chart like this to help you see the results of your survey more clearly.

Music  Fashion  Sport  Wildlife  T.V.  Pets

## TIPS FOR INTERVIEWS AND VISITS

To find out about places to visit or people to interview, look in your local newspaper, phone directory or in books about your local area. The library or tourist office will have leaflets about houses, castles and gardens open to the public, museums, art galleries, theaters, concerts and nature reserves. Why not visit a local factory or supermarket for a story about life "behind the scenes"?

Some useful points to remember:
• You may need to write or phone before you go to ask permission to visit.
• Take a list of questions, notebook, camera and tape recorder (if possible).
• Keep a careful record of everything you see and hear.
• Afterwards write to thank the people who helped you and send them a copy of your article.
• Thank them in the magazine as well.

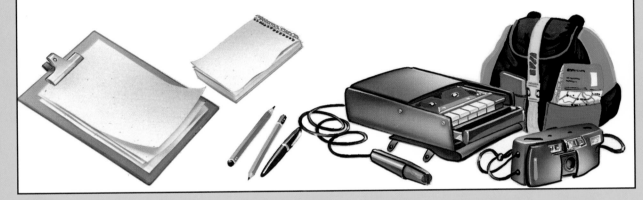

## PICTURE PUZZLES

Picture puzzles should be fun to do but also make readers think a bit to solve them. Here are some ideas:

**Spot the difference**

Finding something in a maze

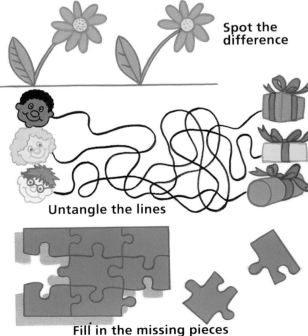

Untangle the lines

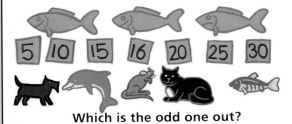

5  10  15  16  20  25  30

Which is the odd one out?

Fill in the missing pieces

## THINGS TO MAKE

You could include step-by-step instructions for making things (see page 21), especially for festivals which happen at certain times of year, like Christmas.

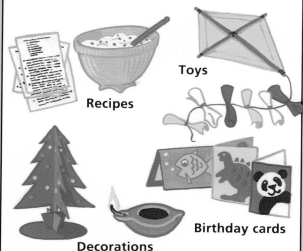

Recipes

Toys

Decorations

Birthday cards

## WORD GAMES

Words don't have to be in straight lines. They can be in a circle, upside down, or in a shape, such as a castle or animal.

The ghost flew round the castle three times...

Soccer has been played in England since the 14th century...

Build up a story or poem by writing words on brick shapes and then shuffling them around.

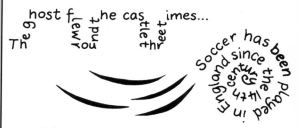

Bubbles
rainbow magic
floating down down
How can we catch them ?

## CLUBS TO JOIN

You can have a club for readers, with a chief in charge of it. Put letters to the chief in the magazine. The club can have competitions, badge

The magazine CLUB

mirror writing

and a secret code.

To make a code, look in a mirror while you write. No one can read this unless they look in a mirror too!

To The Chief
The Magazine Club

To The Chief
The Magazine Club

## CARTOON TRICKS

A simple cartoon should make people laugh, so have a joke in mind while you are scribbling. To help you start, try drawing a shape, such as a triangle, and see what you can turn it into.

Try doodling some lines on a piece of paper. Do they remind you of anything?

# THE WORDS

The words are the nuts and bolts of a magazine – they hold it together. In children's magazines the words come in all shapes and sizes, from small serious words to big, jokey words or words that crawl around the page or leap out at you.

   It is important to match the look of the words with what you are trying to say and the people you are saying it to – your readers. Writing with different pens or brushes can also make the words look different.

## THE FIRST WORDS

Words allow us to communicate with others when we are not there, pass on ideas without making a sound and leave messages for future generations. Writing developed from early picture writing, using symbols to represent ideas, to the alphabets we use today.

**20,000 BC : picture writing on cave walls.**

**3000 BC : wedge-shaped symbols (cuneiform writing) pressed into clay.**

man    horse

ox

**1000 BC : Greek alphabet.**

alpha = A

beta = B

**The Roman alphabet developed from the Greek and is still used in the western world today.**

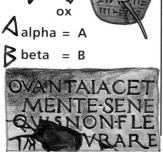

OVANTAIACET
MENTE·SENE
QVISNONFLE
TAVRARE

ZigZag

**Amazing Animals**

• One tooth from an adult elephant weighs more than a brick – 10 pounds.
• Peregrine falcons are the fastest living creatures and can fly at up to 110 mph.
• One ocean sunfish can lay up to 300 million eggs.
• Some whales have voices louder than the sound of a jet plane.

POW!

NEXT MONTH: Holiday Special

Adventure at Sea

Oh no!

There they are

Phew!

**Shapes around cartoon words will reinforce the message.**

**Make the words look different by trying different pens, pencils and brushes.**

# FUN PAGE

## Treasure Island

The words can be stories, poems, quizzes, facts, interviews, jokes, games or cartoon strips.

Try and choose a style of words (type), called a typeface, to suit the message of the words.

## ONE-EYED JACK

One-eyed Jack, the pirate chief,
Was a terrible, fearsome
   ocean thief,
He wore a peg
Upon one leg;
He wore a hook —
And a dirty look!
One eyed Jack, the pirate chief —
A terrible, fearsome ocean thief!

## LETTERS FOR HEADINGS

Readers flip through magazines and glance at the headings to decide what to read. They need to be short and snappy, summarizing an article in a few words. These are some ways to make headings stand out:

Shadows around the letters

3D letters

Wavy or patterned letters

Stick letters

Letters made of dots

Old-fashioned letters

Headings can be curved, or some letters can be bigger than others. They will stand out more if they are on a colored background or have a line underneath.

# TIPS ON WRITING STORIES

Ideas for stories can come to you at any time, so jot them down to use later. Watching people to see how they behave and what they say can give you ideas for characters and plots.

A story can be about people or places you know well, far-away lands, dream worlds or outer space. It can be set in the past, present or future.

Some ideas are: good defeating evil, a search for something, or how a person changes as he or she faces up to problems.

Try to start in an interesting way to catch the reader's attention. Give the plot a beginning, a middle and an end. To help you remember the characters in your story, make cards for each one.

Name: Robomorf (robot)

Age: 1003
Where they live: Zygon12
Appearance: Very tall, green and red striped eyes, black body made of zullite.
Job: Supreme protector to Emperor Polos.

Family and Friends: None, utterly evil.
Special Points: Can change appearance to look like other aliens, can read minds and travel through time.

Name: Rebecca Fox

Age: 10
Where they live: Abbotsville
Appearance: Short, skinny, fair hair (pony tail), blue eyes.
Job: Still at school.

Family and Friends: Lives with mother and brother Sam, best friend Sally.
Special Points: Very bright, but doesn't see point of school. Likes riding.

# THE LOOK OF THE WORDS

There are all sorts of things you can do with words to make them look different. You can make the letters big or small, write them in small letters (lower case), CAPITAL LETTERS (upper case) or SMALL CAPITALS.

You can change the amount of space between the lines, the words or even the i n d i v i d u a l  l e t t e r s. Words can be **bold**, *italic* or Roman.

Conversations go in speech bubbles.

**Recipes, notes or labels around pictures can be hand-written.**

Banana Cake

Ingredients
1¾ cups mashed bananas    ½ cup raisins
1 cup walnuts    1 cup rolled oats
¼ cup cooking oil    1¼ cups flour
    pinch of salt

Method
① Heat oven to 375°F (190°C)
② Mix ingredients together and spoon into a bread pan
③ Bake for about an hour.

**Funny poems, jokes or special competitions can be in jazzy type.**

I always eat peas with honey,
I've done so all my life
They do taste kind of funny
But it keeps them on the knife.

**For serious information or facts and figures, the words need to be clear and easy to read.**

The spiral track on a compact disc is thinner than a human hair and about 3 miles long.

**Crickets have ears on their knees.**

The Colosseum in Rome once had enough seats for 50,000 people.

## WORD PICTURES

You could make up your own picture symbols to stand for different words. If you tell members of the magazine club what the symbols mean, you could use them like a secret code. The club members will be the only people who understand the messages in the magazine.

meet me

after school

to play football

## CARTOON WORDS

The shape of speech bubbles can be important. Straight lines suggest fierce words. Thought clouds tell you what a character is thinking. Loud noises are often inside star shapes. If the letters overlap, it suggests movement.

## MISTAKES AND CHANGES

Magazine editors have to check that the words are spelled correctly and are easy to read. They make sure that the meaning is clear. Editors also check the words are arranged properly on the page next to the right pictures and that the words fit in the space available.

To save time, editors use a series of symbols to stand for any changes they need to make. You can see some of them below. They usually make one mark near the words and another in the margin. The typesetters then make the changes to the words when they set the text – see page 34 for more about typesetting.

| Text mark | Margin mark | Meaning |
|---|---|---|
| / through letters or ⊢ through words | ⌀ | Delete |
| ⋀ | New text followed by ⋀ | Insert the new text in the margin |
| ⊔⊓ | ⊔⊓ | Transpose (change round) |
| Ī | ⌀ | Delete and close up |

To help rare animals ~~to~~ survive, ⌀
we can stop destroying their
*and* habitats ⋀ set aside more areas
of land and water as nature
⌀ *We can* reserves ⋀ *we can* stop buying goods made
from rare animals and cut down
on the amount of pollution in ⌀

## BEAUTIFUL WRITING

The sort of writing in this box is called calligraphy. It is more like drawing than writing and is often used for decoration. To make the thick and thin strokes of the letters, you need a pen with a broad, square end. Hold the pen at an angle of about 30 degrees to the page. Practice to get it right. Writing on faint pencil lines will help you get the letters straight and space them out evenly.

**Fountain pens**

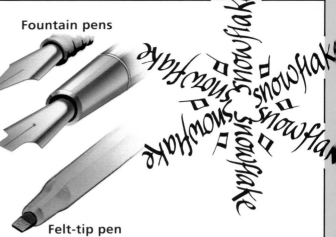

**Felt-tip pen**

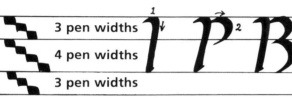

3 pen widths

4 pen widths

3 pen widths

abcdefghijklm
nopqrstuvwxyz

ABCDEFGHIJKLMNOPQRSTUVWXYZ

## ILLUMINATED LETTERS

In medieval times, scribes in monasteries often decorated or "illuminated" the first letter on a page, a paragraph or a chapter with patterns or pictures. You could try decorating the first letters of some of your magazine articles like this.

## BRUSH STROKES

In China, brushes have been used for calligraphy for thousands of years. In Chinese, each character stands for a single word which was originally based on a picture. These changed over the years to become simple brush strokes.

**The brush is held vertically, like this.**

**How the Chinese word for tree developed**

Picture          Symbol

## MAKE A QUILL PEN

To make a quill pen, you need a turkey, hen or crow feather, a sharp knife and a needle. Ask an adult to help you.

### How to make it

**1** Hold the feather and cut off the tip so it is about 8 inches long. Cut off the side pieces.

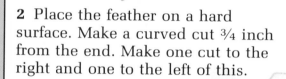

**2** Place the feather on a hard surface. Make a curved cut ¾ inch from the end. Make one cut to the right and one to the left of this.

**3** Dig out the "pith" with the needle.

**4** Put the quill on a hard surface. Cut a square end and a slit near this for the ink to flow down.

**Brush a small amount of ink onto the end of your quill. Press lightly to start writing.**

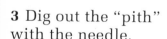

## DID YOU KNOW?

Different styles of alphabets are called typefaces. There are thousands of them. Some are named after the people who invented them, such as Eric Gill. Others have unusual names, such as Bottleneck or Superstar. Try designing your own typeface for your magazine.

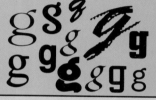

**LMW**
**Y S N**
**P N**
**R**

**Typefaces can be serif or sans (without) serif. Serifs are the strokes which finish off the ends of the letters.**

**Look at the small 'g' to spot differences between typefaces.**

## RUBBINGS

You can create interesting letters or numbers by taking rubbings with a crayon. Look for letters on stone buildings, car number plates or coins. Put a piece of clean paper over the letters and rub lightly with the crayon until the letters show up.

**You can cut letters or numbers out of the rubbings and arrange them to make new words or numbers.**

# THE PICTURES

From paintings and cartoons to photographs and sketches, pictures brighten up a magazine and make it special. It's important to match up the look or style of the pictures with what the words are saying. Straightforward diagrams or maps make it easier to understand facts or explain how to make something. Cartoons add a sense of fun and adventure, while photographs show readers what something or someone is really like.

### BIGGER OR SMALLER?

The pictures for magazines are often drawn larger than the size they need to be. This helps the artist to include details. When the drawings are reduced, they look crisper. Artwork is scaled up or down (reduced or enlarged) by drawing a diagonal line across it. The ratio of the vertical to the horizontal stays the same.

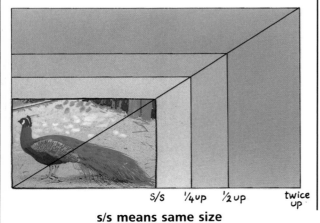

s/s    ¼ up    ½ up     twice up

**s/s means same size**

Drawings or sketches show what a story, poem, competition, puzzle or game is about. They can be serious or funny, happy or sad, in all kinds of styles.

Cartoons suggest jokes, events and happenings with just a simple drawing. Some cartoons do not need words to go with the pictures.

WHOOSH!

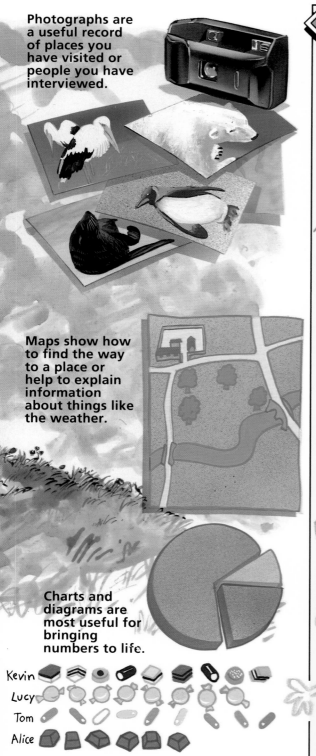

Photographs are a useful record of places you have visited or people you have interviewed.

Maps show how to find the way to a place or help to explain information about things like the weather.

Charts and diagrams are most useful for bringing numbers to life.

Kevin

Lucy

Tom

Alice

Sweets eaten this week

## CARTOONS

The main point in a cartoon is to draw simply and very clearly. Practise drawing how people move by sketching stick figures in different positions. You can work these up into more finished drawings and add detail.

Faces are very important in cartoons. Start a face with a balloon shape and put the eyes, nose and mouth in different places to suggest different moods. Try changing the shape of the head too.

smug face    clever face

machine head

lively head

speed lines

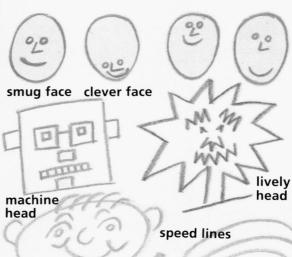

## FROM SKETCH TO ARTWORK

Most artists start with sketches, or roughs, before they do the painting or drawing ("artwork"). They may draw people in different positions or faces with different expressions. Then they add details and may send their roughs off for checking. If people do artwork for your magazine, remember it's easier to make roughs.

## CHOOSING THE RIGHT STYLE

**A detailed style using soft pencils and shadows makes a picture thoughtful and sensitive.**

Some artists draw in a variety of different styles; others specialize in their own particular style. Before you choose someone to draw pictures for your magazine, ask several people to show you some examples of their work or do a piece of sample artwork. Then pick the one which best matches the words that will go with the pictures.

**Water colors give a drawing soft edges and can suggest moods and feelings in some detail.**

**A loose, but realistic, style using brush and ink gives an immediate, lively feel.**

**A simple cartoon style with bright colors and black outlines will suit a funny story.**

## STEP-BY-STEP

If you need to explain how to make something, it's best to break down the instructions into a number of simple steps. Try to place the words next to the pictures they are describing instead of putting them in a big block. Readers won't bother to wade through lots of words to find out what to do. Words and pictures need to work well together.

**Include a list of "what you need" so readers can collect these things before they start.**

**Divide up the instructions into several steps and number each one clearly.**

**Include close-ups to make any complicated instructions easier to follow.**

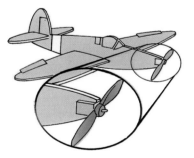

**Use labels and lines to draw attention to details so the words are right next to the relevant part of the pictures.**

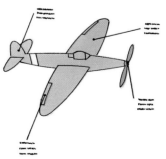

## DIAGRAMS AND MAPS

A lot of information is easier to understand in a picture rather than in words or numbers. A complicated explanation of how something works will be helped by a sketch that makes the main point easier to understand. If you are describing how to get to a place, a map is clearer and more accurate than a lot of words.

**Pie charts or bar charts make it easier to compare numbers and see the results of a survey at a glance.**

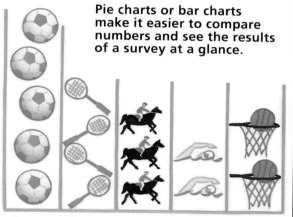

Soccer  Tennis  Riding  Swimming  Basketball

**A picture is more use than thousands of words. This one shows global warming!**

**Grid lines on maps help you to give an accurate reference to a place. You need to follow one line from the top or bottom of the map, and one from side to side, and see where they cross.**

# TRACING PHOTOGRAPHS

Tracing a picture from a photo is an easy way to get an accurate drawing.

Go over the tracing afterwards with ink or felt pen.

**1** Trace the outline, leaving out details and shadows.

**2** Scribble over the back of the outline with a soft pencil.

**3** Turn the tracing over, tape it on to clean paper and go over the outline with a hard pencil.

---

## TIPS FOR TAKING PHOTOGRAPHS

- Before taking a photo, check if you need permission. Keep a note of where and when you take each one and what it is about.
- Don't stand too far away from the object or person you are photographing.
- Keep the light behind you.
- Hold the camera steady – balance it on a wall or a post if necessary.
- Take lots of photographs from different angles so you will have plenty to choose from.
- Black and white photographs are clear and good for reference.

## PHOTOGRAPHS OR DRAWINGS?

Photographs and drawings each have their plus and minus points. Think about the message you are trying to put across and choose whichever suits that best. Here are a few points to consider:

| PHOTOGRAPH | DRAWING |
|---|---|
|  |  |
| shows real people and places and is accurate | is only a copy and depends on the artist |
| hard to use it to show how things work | can show inside something and how it works |
| usually has a lot of detail and background | can highlight one thing and leave out details |
| limited choice of shapes, but you can cut out part of it | can be any shape and fill the space available |
| limited range of styles | many different styles |

## SPRAY PAINTING

This is a good way to make clear shapes and create faded effects. You can use spray paints from aerosol cans, but make sure they are ozone-friendly!

**1** Draw a shape on some thin card.

**2** Cut out the shape, leaving the edges as clear as you can. This is called a "mask".

**3** Put the card on a piece of paper. Tape down the edges.

**4** Spray paint in the hole in the card.

**5** Carefully remove the mask when the paint is dry.

## ? DID YOU KNOW?

Cartoons were originally sketches made before an artist started the finished work, such as paintings, tapestries or mosaics. Nowadays, a cartoon is a drawing in its own right and is often funny. Cartoonists may comment on famous people by drawing exaggerated portraits ("caricatures").

A cartoon strip is a series of pictures telling a story. It often involves a superhero who has a special ability.

## MAKE A FILING SYSTEM

It is easy to lose track of the pictures you collect for your magazine. They may fall behind cupboards or get buried in a drawer. But if you make a filing system, you will be able to keep the pictures safely and find them when you need them.

**Divide sections with cardboard.**

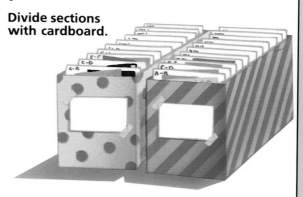

**Use cardboard from large, empty boxes. Label each divider. Make sections according to letters of the alphabet or the type of picture.**

Artwork can easily be creased or torn or have drinks spilled on it. Make covers for it from tracing paper with a layer of thicker paper on top, or put it in plastic bags for extra protection.

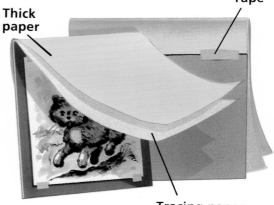

Thick paper

Tape

Tracing paper

# THE DESIGN

Design is all about arranging things on the page so they are easy to read and good to look at. The design should also match the content. It can be free and open for jokey or fun pages, but straighter and more formal for serious information or facts.

Decide how important items are, and the best order to put them in. See if there is anything that needs to be separated out in a box. Don't feel you have to squash everything in. If there is not enough space, leave something out. You may need to re-draw your design several times before it looks right.

## COMPUTER DESIGN

Professional designers often use computers to design magazine pages. They move the actual words and pictures about on the screen until they feel the design works. This is quicker and more accurate than drawing and positioning everything by hand. It is also much easier to make changes and fit text around pictures.

**You may be able to try some desk-top publishing for yourself.**

Here are three ways of designing the same page. Which one do you think works best? Can you work out other designs?

Things to fit in:

How to make something

End of a story and a picture

A quiz

**The process of arranging words and pictures on a page is called layout. It is helpful to base this on a grid (see page 26), to make it accurate.**

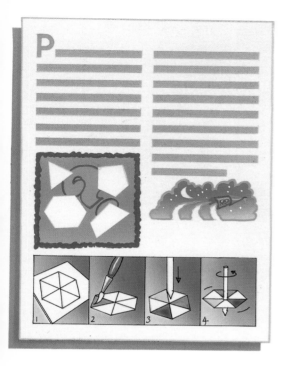

## DRAW A STORYBOARD

Before you design your magazine, it's a good idea to draw a plan (called a "storyboard") of the pages, so you can see them all at a glance. It helps you arrange everything, so you won't run out of space or have any blank pages. You can also draw a storyboard to show other people what your magazine will look like.

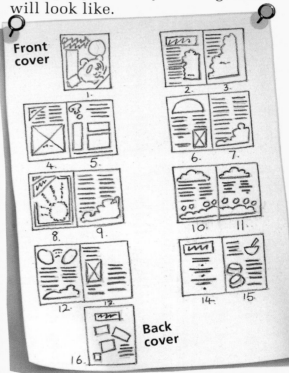

On a large piece of paper, draw a little box for every two pages, called a "spread." Write the page numbers, called "folios," underneath. Sketch roughly in pencil where the words and pictures will go. You can always rub things out and make changes later.

## STAGES IN DESIGN

**1** Divide up the words into chunks according to their importance and which pictures they go with.
**2** Then draw small sketches to work out different ways of arranging the words and pictures on the page. These are called thumbnail sketches.

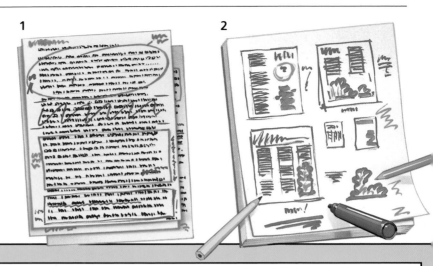

## DRAW A GRID

A grid is a framework for each double page, called a spread. It helps designers work out where to put the words and pictures without having to measure everything every time. Grids are often drawn in light blue, which will not show up during copying or printing. You can draw up one grid and put it under tracing paper or thin white paper each time. Or you can make several photocopies from the original grid. Magazines often have grids with three columns because there is a lot to fit on each page. It is best to keep the words inside the lines of the grid, but the pictures can break out. This makes the page look lively and interesting.

Trim marks show edge of the page.

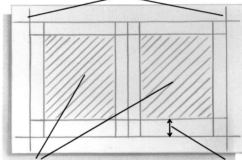

Words and pictures go in shaded areas.

Center fold mark, called the gutter.

Bottom margin — usually bigger than top or side margins.

Text lines.

Grid lines to divide pages.

Line for page number, called a folio.

**3**

**3** When you are happy with one design, you may want to draw it full size to check that it works.

**4** A detailed design, called a visual, will help you to convince people to accept your design.

**4**

## DESIGN TIPS

Good design works when the different elements fit together and don't fight with each other.

* Leave enough space for the words so they are clear and easy to read.

* The words and pictures should work together and it should be obvious which words go with which picture.

* Change the design for new stories or articles to make the magazine look lively and exciting.

* Make the pages full and busy, but leave some white space.

## BOXES AND BORDERS

Colorful or patterned borders make the pages look fun. They can also give information; for example, a line of question marks tells the readers about a quiz. Try using different patterns, such as stripes and zigzags, and experiment with different materials.

Use boxes to separate information which does not fit in with the rest of the page or to make it look important.

# DESIGN A GAME

Games work best if they have a purpose or a theme, such as "Who can eat the most?" or "Who can escape from the dinosaur first?" They need to have a clearly marked start and finish and a set of rules for how to play the game. Include special "problem" or "bonus" squares every so often to make players go back or forward more than one square. This makes the game longer.

Many games involve throwing dice to move counters from one square to another.

**You could base the game on a board of squares, like a chessboard. Draw pictures in the squares if you like.**

Finish — Back 4 places — 33 32 31 — Go to finish
24 25 — Back 6 places — 27 28 29
Move to 30! — 22 21 20 19 18
12 — Throw again — 14 15 16 — Move on 7 squares
11 10 9 — Go back to start — 7 6
Start — 1 2 3 — Move on 2 squares — 5

**Or you could arrange the squares in a bold shape, such as a zig-zag. Number each square clearly so the order is obvious.**

1 2 3 4 5 6 7 8 9 10 11 12 13 14 15 16 17 18 END

**RULES**
"Who can eat the most?" Throw 6 to start. Throw again to see how far to move. The person who lands on the most food squares wins.

END — 36 35 34 33 32 31 30 29 28 27 26 25 24 23 22 21 20 19 18 17 16 15 14 13 12 11 10 9 8 7 6 5 4 3 2 1 — START

Swing over river on a creeper – go to end!

Extra turn

Chased by tyrannosaurus – go back to ②

Fall over sleeping dinosaur – miss a turn

Get a ride on a brontosaurus go to ③⓪

Fall into river – miss a turn

Take short cut – go on to ⑫

**An animal outline makes a good shape for a game. You can use any shape for the steps in the game – circles, diamonds and so on.**

## MAKE A FLIP STRIP

To make your magazine a bit different, why not include a flip strip in one corner of the pages? As readers flip the pages, the picture in the strip will look as if it is moving. It's best to choose a simple event, such as a flower opening or a bird flying.

Films are made up of a series of still pictures like these. But they use so many pictures – 24 a second – that our eyes cannot pick out each one, so the pictures seem to be moving.

Draw a series of pictures, but make each one only slightly different from the one before.

Position the pictures carefully, so that each one is in exactly the same position on every page.

**First picture in sequence**

**Last picture in sequence**

## DESIGN A SYMBOL

Ask an expert

Story

Quiz

Color-it-in

Game

Things to make

Try inventing little symbols for the different items in your magazine. These will help readers to pick out the different items on each page and find the ones they are most interested in.

Symbols are especially useful if the pages of your magazine are crowded and busy. Keep the symbols simple and concentrate on the main point. Use bold lines and bright colors to make them stand out well.

Turn over to find out how to put your magazine together.

# THE COVER

The front cover is one of the most important parts of a magazine. It needs to be eye-catching and stand out well from a distance. It needs to look different from all the other magazines so people can recognize it easily. And it needs to tell readers what's inside and why your magazine is better than all the others. To persuade people to buy magazines, there are often free gifts stuck to the cover.

## THE BACK COVER

It's a good idea to make the most of the back cover so you don't waste valuable space. This is often a good place for readers' letters or a special competition. It could also be used to tell readers what is coming up in the next issue. If you have sponsors who are helping to pay for your magazine, they may want to advertise on the back cover. If you can't think of anything else, have a big picture — whatever you do, don't leave the back cover blank!

For the title, use large letters that are an interesting shape and overlap them or put them at an angle.

Colorful borders make the title stand out.

Use one big picture, such as a face, for maximum impact.

If you charge for your magazine, the price should be easy to find.

Make a short list of what's inside. Use large dots, called bullets, to highlight each item.

Everyone likes to get something for nothing, so a free gift is sure to win over new readers.

50¢
June 1993
Issue 4

IN THIS MONTH'S

OK!

- PANDAS
- Star Interview
- JOKES
- Games
- FACT PAGE
- Quiz
- POST BAG
and
FREE GIFT

OK!

Leave space for the date and number of the issue.

A brightly colored corner, called a flash, draws attention to something special.

OK!

Cut-out mobile on page 4

## FREE GIFTS

The best things to give away with your magazine are small objects such as buttons, stencils, transfers or stickers. Fix them to the front of the magazine with clear sticky tape.

## MAKE A BUTTON
### WHAT YOU NEED

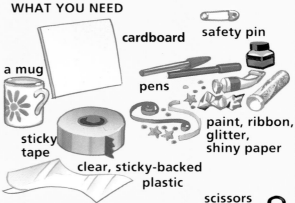

cardboard

safety pin

a mug

pens

paint, ribbon, glitter, shiny paper

sticky tape

clear, sticky-backed plastic

scissors

### How to make it

**1** Use a pencil to draw around the bottom of a mug to make a circle.
**2** Cut out the circle.
**3** Decorate the front of the circle and write a message in the middle.
**4** Tape a safety pin on the back.
**5** Stretch the clear plastic over the front to protect the button from dirt and scratches.

1  2  3

Choose an important issue or just a fun message.

Save the Forests

I ♥ PANDAS

Wicked

31

# MAKING THE MAGAZINE

Once you have collected all the words and pictures for your magazine, and designed the pages, the next step is to decide how many copies you want to make. You could make just one copy – in a big scrapbook, for instance – and pass it around. Or you could print several copies. Printing is a way of making the same image appear on a surface (such as paper) over and over again without having to re-draw it each time. You could print your magazine on a photocopier, use a desk-top publishing system or take it to a print shop. Most magazines are held together with staples, but you could sew the pages together or use plastic binders.

## COPYING BY HAND

Before printing was invented, everything had to be written and copied by hand. In Christian countries, specially trained monks copied page after page in a room called a scriptorium. They used quill pens and the whole process took a long time.

Photocopy your magazine on colored paper to make it look more interesting.

hole punch

ribbons and shoelaces

needles

strong thread

long-arm stapler

32

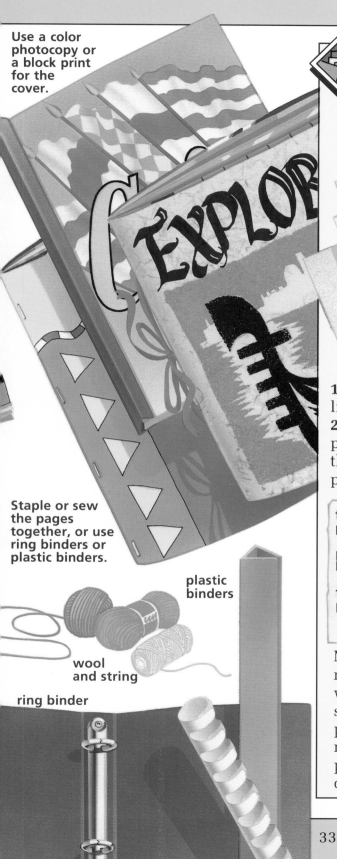

Use a color photocopy or a block print for the cover.

Staple or sew the pages together, or use ring binders or plastic binders.

plastic binders

wool and string

ring binder

**WHAT YOU NEED**
paper of different colors, texture and thicknesses, pens, brushes, ink and paint.

You can try to match the type of paper with the words and pictures on the page.

**1** On each piece of paper, draw a line with each pen and brush.
**2** See how the paper soaks up the paint or ink. Do the lines show through the paper? Does colored paper look better?

felt-tip pen

paint brush

fountain pen

Most paper today is made by mixing mashed up wood and water with chemicals. The chemicals very slowly eat the paper away and the paper destroys itself. Older paper, made from animal skins, rags, or papyrus, does not contain these chemicals, so it lasts much longer.

## D.I.Y. TYPE

If you don't want to write your magazine by hand, try the ideas shown here. Sheets of instant transfer lettering or rubbings of letters (see page 17) are useful. Use pencil guide lines to help you get the words straight.

A typewriter or word processor will make the words look professional.

Rub the letters off sheet with a pencil.

Cut out letters from rubbings of coins and inscriptions, and paste down.

A typewriter carbon ribbon makes letters thicker and blacker.

Use a word processor and printer for the words. Add pictures later.

On a poor-quality printer, you can see the dots which make up the letters.

Unit
Tele
Post

A good quality printer doesn't show the dots.

Unit
Tele
Post

## TYPESETTING

The words or type in magazines in the shops are produced on machines which make and arrange the type. This is called typesetting. The first typesetting used movable metal letters. In the 1950s, phototypesetting machines set type photographically. Modern typesetting uses computers, lasers and photography.

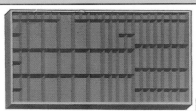

case for storing metal letters

letters placed in order in a composing stick

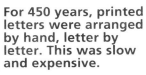

For 450 years, printed letters were arranged by hand, letter by letter. This was slow and expensive.

The letter stands up from one of a stick of metal.

In computer typesetting, the machine stores letters as codes of numbers (digital codes). These are decoded and reproduced by computer-controlled lasers.

Each letter is stored as a series of tiny dots. Each dot has a coded number.

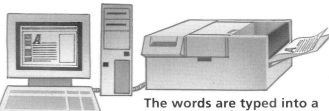

The words are typed into a computer and any changes are made on the screen. Then they are typeset.

## ? DID YOU KNOW?

The Chinese invented movable type in 1041. They made the letters from baked clay. Metal type was first made in Korea in the early 1400's.

## D.I.Y. PRINTING

To print copies of your magazine, first stick down the words and pictures in position on large, flat sheets of paper.

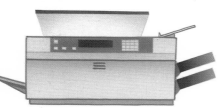

**Libraries and instant print shops have photocopiers the public can pay to use. Photocopies can be up to 11 by 17 inches.**

**To make a block print, carefully use a knife and gouge to cut the picture into the linoleum block. Roll ink over it and press paper on top.**

**Print shops will be able to advise you on the printing process. You may be able to find a sponsor or someone advertising in the magazine to pay for the printing.**

## THE PRINTING PROCESS

Color pictures in a magazine are made up of lots of dots. You can see these through a magnifying glass. Four colors (yellow, red, blue, and black) are used and mixed to make other colors. A computerized machine called a scanner makes a piece of film for each of the four colors.

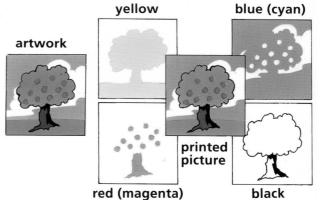

artwork

yellow

blue (cyan)

red (magenta)

black

printed picture

**The scanner calculates how many dots are needed to reproduce each of the four colors.**

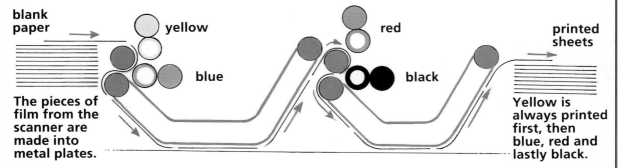

blank paper

yellow

blue

red

black

printed sheets

**The pieces of film from the scanner are made into metal plates.**

**Yellow is always printed first, then blue, red and lastly black.**

**The plates are wrapped around cylinders on a machine called a printing press. The cylinders are inked with yellow, blue, red or black ink. As sheets of blank paper travel through the machine, the image on the cylinders is printed on the paper.**

## MAKE A STENCIL

**2** A cardboard stencil will easily go soggy and fall apart. So tape shiny paper, thin plastic or stencil paper over the cardboard and carefully cut out the letters.

These parts are called bridges. They keep the stencil from falling apart.

### How to make it

**1** Carefully draw or trace the letters you want on to a piece of thick card.

**3** Use a stiff brush to dab paint through the stencil on to a piece of clean paper. Take care not to smudge the letters when you remove the stencil afterwards.

## BLOCK PRINTING

Try making a printing block from a smooth ceiling tile – the kind sold in D.I.Y. shops. Choose one which has a smooth surface.

### How to make it

**1** Draw a picture lightly on the tile with a felt-tip pen. Then go over it with a sharp pencil to press the lines into the surface of the tile.

**2** Soak a printing roller (from an art shop) evenly with ink and roll the ink over the tile. The design will show up white.

ceiling tile

printing roller

printing ink

**3** Place the tile face down on a sheet of paper. Roll a clean roller over the top to print the picture on the paper.

ceiling tile

paper

clean roller

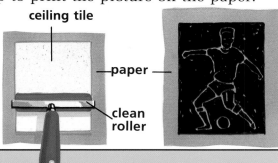

felt-tip pen          sharp pencil

## FOLDING THE PAGES

On a printing press, magazines are printed on huge sheets of paper. The pages have to be arranged in certain positions so they are in the right order when they are cut and folded. They are often arranged in sections of 8, 16 or 32 pages. Each section is called a signature.

Here is one way of arranging pages on both sides of a large sheet of paper to make a 16 page magazine. Fasten the pages together and cut them open afterwards.

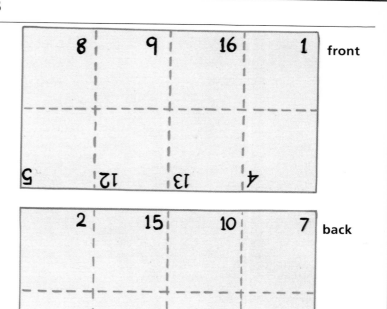

front

back

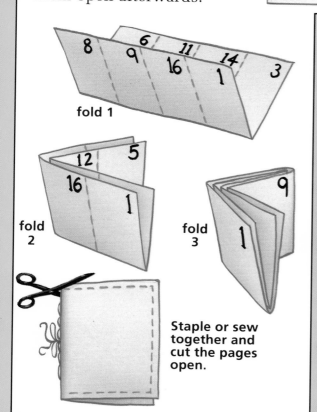

fold 1

fold 2

fold 3

Staple or sew together and cut the pages open.

## MAKE A POSTER MAGAZINE

One way of making a magazine without stapling or sewing the pages together is to produce a poster magazine. This is made from one large sheet of paper, with a poster on one side and all the other pages and covers on the other side. Look at the diagram on the right to see how to arrange the pages. You need to fold the sheet three times along the lines marked, so that only the front and back covers can be seen when it is folded.

This sort of magazine does not have many pages, so it is quick to make. It works best if it is about one theme, such as soccer or music.

**very large sheet of paper**

**on one side**

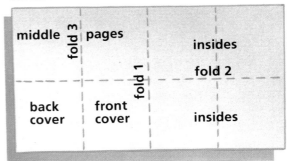

middle pages · fold 3 · insides · fold 2 · fold 1 · back cover · front cover · insides

**on the other side**

**a large poster**

**How to fold**

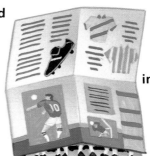

insides

## MAKE A SCRAPBOOK MAGAZINE

If you can't print lots of copies of your magazine, make one special issue instead. Use glue or tape to stick the words, photographs and drawings in a big scrapbook. You can add borders or rules afterwards. Write the page numbers in one corner. Then pass the magazine around your friends.

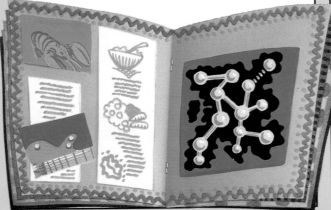

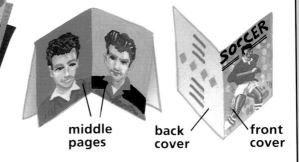

middle pages · back cover · front cover

## KEEPING THE PAGES TOGETHER

If you make your magazine from loose pages, you need to staple or sew them. Sewing will make the magazine stronger so it doesn't fall apart easily, especially if there is just one copy to pass around.

folded pages sewn together

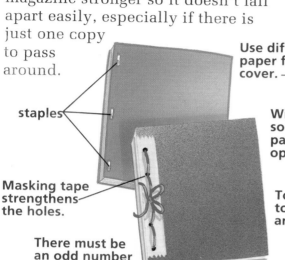

staples

Use different paper for the cover.

With a plastic binder you lose some of each page and the pages don't lie flat when you open the magazine.

Masking tape strengthens the holes.

There must be an odd number of holes.

To sew the pages together start here and follow arrows.

Tie the ends together.

## MAKE A FOLDER

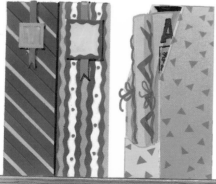

### How to make it

**1** Find a large cereal box.
**2** Cut off most of one of the long, thin sides and part of the top, as shown.
**3** Make a tag from the stiff paper and write the issue numbers on it.
**4** Fix the tag to a piece of ribbon and tape this to the other side of the box.
**5** Decorate the sides of the box with wrapping paper or color it in with your own design.

**WHAT YOU NEED**

wrapping paper

ribbon

scissors

empty cereal box

sticky tape

cut here

numbers of issues

# FROM START TO FINISH

Creating your own magazine involves all sorts of skills, from writing, drawing and making things, to interviewing people and sorting out ideas and information. So you can choose to work on the things you are good at, and how much or how little you want to do. You may want to be in charge of everything, or just write or draw something every so often. When you're working on one issue, try to think ahead and plan the contents of the next three or four issues.

## PUBLICITY

Remember to tell people why they should read your magazine and how they can get hold of a copy. Make a list of the most interesting features to mention. You could even have a party when the first issue is ready, to show people what you are doing and what your plans are for the future.

Try making a poster to advertise the first issue of the magazine, or to tell people about special free gifts or competitions.

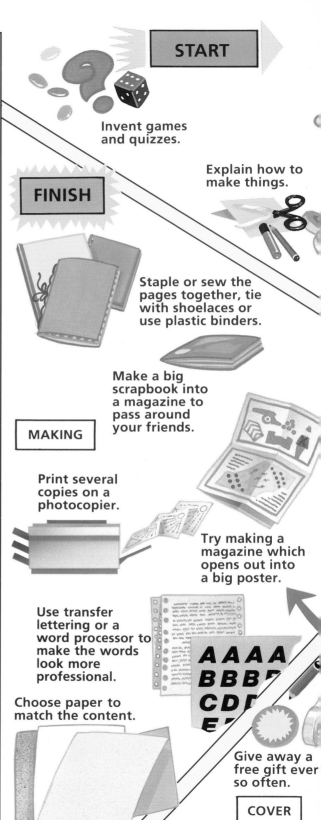

**START**

Invent games and quizzes.

Explain how to make things.

**FINISH**

Staple or sew the pages together, tie with shoelaces or use plastic binders.

Make a big scrapbook into a magazine to pass around your friends.

**MAKING**

Print several copies on a photocopier.

Try making a magazine which opens out into a big poster.

Use transfer lettering or a word processor to make the words look more professional.

Choose paper to match the content.

Give away a free gift ever so often.

**COVER**

## IDEAS

Write down ideas so you won't forget them.

Experiment with different pens, pencils and brushes.

## WORDS

Choose a typeface which matches the words.

Write stories and poems.

Interview people and visit places of interest.

Make cards to help you remember the characters in a story.

Create cartoons for adventure stories.

Draw diagrams to explain how things work.

# HOW TO CREATE YOUR OWN MAGAZINE

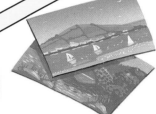

Take photographs of people and places.

## PICTURES

Paint pictures to go with stories or poems.

For the title of the magazine, choose big, bold letters and shapes.

Use a grid to make sure everything is in the right position.

Put letters from readers on the back cover.

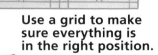

Make up patterned borders for pages or boxes.

Plan the pages on a storyboard.

## DESIGN

# GLOSSARY

**Alphabet**   A set of letters, numbers and punctuation marks used in a language.

**Artwork**   Pictures or lettering or both of these, ready to send to the printers to be reproduced.

**Bold type**   Thicker letters used to emphasize words by making them stand out.

**Box rule**   A line drawn around words or pictures or both of these.

**Bullets**   Dots used to highlight and draw attention to points in the text.

**Calligraphy**   "Beautiful writing," which is often very elaborate and used for decorative effect.

**Caption**   Text about an illustration or a photograph.

**Cartoon**   A particular kind of drawing using a few bold lines. It is often very funny, or pokes fun at the way people look or the things they say.

**Codex**   An ancient document written on a long strip of paper and folded up flat.

**Composing stick**   A long wooden bar held in the hand and used to assemble the metal letters in hot metal typesetting.

**Cuneiform writing**   Wedge-shaped writing on baked clay tablets used in ancient inscriptions of Assyria and Persia (modern-day Syria and Iran).

**Digital typesetting**   Typesetting in which the letters are built up from number codes in a computer. It also involves lasers and photography.

**Folio**   Page number.

**Grid**   A framework of lines marking the columns and margins of a page. It is used to position words and pictures accurately on a page.

**Gutter**   The center line of a double-page spread.

**Heading**   Word or words which introduce the content of a page, a chapter, a poster, a box and so on.

**Hot metal typesetting**   Reproducing letters by using molten metal letters, which have to be assembled by hand.

**Illuminated letters**   Those from medieval manuscripts which are decorated with patterns, pictures and borders.

**Illustration**   Picture drawn by hand, rather than a photograph taken by a machine.

**Italic**   Type of handwriting or printed lettering which slopes to the right.

**Label**   A very short caption, often with an arrow or lead line pointing directly to something. It is sometimes called a call-out.

**Layout**   A plan showing the positions and arrangement of words and pictures on a page.

**Lower case**   Small letters.

**Magazine**   A publication which appears at regular intervals. It is usually illustrated and contains the work of several different writers.

**Margin**   The blank areas around the words and pictures on a page.

**Marking up**   Writing instructions on the text for the typesetter to follow.

**Paste-up**   The process of sticking the text and pictures in the correct position ready to be reproduced and printed.

**Phototypesetting**   Reproducing letters by setting type photographically on paper.

**Quill pen**   A pen made from the hollow central shaft of a bird's feather.

**Sans serif**   A plain letter without curly or twirly strokes.

**Scriptorium**   A special room in a medieval monastery where scribes copied books and documents by hand.

**Serifs**   The strokes which finish off the ends of the arms, stems and curves of letters.

**Spread**   Two pages side by side.

**Stencil**   A picture or letters cut out of a surface which can be reproduced by painting or drawing through the holes.

**Storyboard**   A page plan of a whole magazine drawn up as a series of double-page spreads on a very small scale.

**Text**   The words, which are sometimes also called copy.

**Thumbnail**   Tiny sketch drawn in proportion to the full-size work. Used to work out the different ways of arranging words and pictures on a page.

**Trim marks**   The marks outside the page area showing where the paper will be cut.

**Typeface**   The name for a particular design of type.

**Typesetting**   Arranging or "setting" letters to form words and sentences in the right order and with the correct spaces between them.

**Upper case**   Capital letters.

**Visual**   A well-worked out design, sometimes in color, which gives a good idea of the finished work.

# INDEX